3103 2849  '84

The
Essentials
of MLA Style

The
Essentials
of MLA Style

A Guide to the System of
Documentation Recommended
by the MLA for Writers
of Research Papers

with an Appendix on APA Style

Joseph F. Trimmer

Houghton Mifflin Company
Boston   New York

This book reprints the text of *A Guide to MLA Documentation*, 4th Edition, by Joseph F. Trimmer, published by Houghton Mifflin Company in 1996. Published by arrangement with the College Division of Houghton Mifflin Company.

This guide in part summarizes the documentation style of the Modern Language Association of America as it appears in the *MLA Handbook for Writers of Research Papers*, 4th ed., by Joseph Gibaldi (New York: MLA, 1995). This guide is not a work of the Modern Language Association of America, however, and bears no endorsement from the association. For a fuller presentation of many of the topics covered in this guide, readers should consult the *MLA Handbook*.

For information about permission to reproduce selections from this book, write to College Permissions, Houghton Mifflin Company, 222 Berkeley Street, Boston, Massachusetts 02116.

Library of Congress Cataloging-in-Publication Data
Trimmer, Joseph F.
    [Guide to MLA documentation]
    The essentials of MLA style : a guide to the system of documentation recommended by the MLA for writers of research papers, with an Appendix on APA style / Joseph F. Trimmer.
        p.   cm.
    Originally published: A guide to MLA documentation, 4th ed., 1996.
    Includes index
    ISBN 0-395-88316-4
    1. Authorship — Style manuals. 2. Scholarly publishing — Handbooks, manuals, etc. I. Title.
    PN147.T75 1998
    808'.027— dc21   97-53060 CIP

Printed in the United States of America

QUM 10

First Houghton Mifflin trade paperback edition 1998

Contents

The
Essentials
of **MLA Style**

Preface

This book explains the style recommended by the Modern Language Association (MLA) for documenting sources in research papers. It also analyzes some of the implications of MLA style for your research and composing. More detailed information is given in the *MLA Handbook*.

MLA style has three major features. First, all sources cited in a paper are listed in a section entitled **Works Cited**, which is located at the end of the paper. Second, material borrowed from another source is documented within the text by a brief parenthetical reference that directs readers to the full citation in the list of works cited. Third, numbered footnotes or endnotes are used to present two types of supplementary information: (1) commentary or explanation that the text cannot accommodate and (2) bibliographical notes that contain several source citations.

1. Preparing the List of Works Cited

I n a research paper that follows MLA style, the list of works cited is the *only* place where readers will find complete information about the sources you have cited. For that reason, your list must be thorough and accurate.

The list of works cited appears at the end of your paper and, as its title suggests, lists only the works you have cited in your paper. Occasionally, your instructor may ask you to prepare a list of works consulted. That list would include not only the sources you cite but also the sources you consulted as you conducted your research. In either case, MLA prefers Works Cited or Works Consulted to the more limited heading Bibliography (literally, "description of books") because those headings are more likely to accommodate the variety of sources—articles, films, computer software—that writers may cite in a research paper.

To prepare the list of works cited, follow these general guidelines:

1. Paginate the works cited section as a continuation of your text. If the text of your paper ends on page 8, begin your list on page 9 (unless there is an intervening page of endnotes).
2. Double-space successive lines of an entry and between entries.
3. Begin the first line of an entry flush left, and indent successive lines five spaces or one-half inch.

4. List entries in alphabetical order according to the last name of the author.

5. If you are listing more than one work by the same author, alphabetize the works according to title (excluding the articles *a, an,* and *the*). Instead of repeating the author's name, type *three* hyphens and a period, then give the title.

6. Underline the titles of works published independently— books, plays, long poems, pamphlets, periodicals, films.

7. Although you do not *need* to underline the spaces between words, a continuous line is easier to type and guarantees that all features of the title are underlined. Type a continuous line under titles unless you are instructed to do otherwise.

8. If you are citing a book whose title includes the title of another book, underline the main title, but do not underline the other title (for example, A Casebook on Ralph Ellison's Invisible Man).

9. Use quotation marks to indicate the titles of short works that appear in larger works (for example, "Minutes of Glory." African Short Stories). Also use quotation marks for song titles and for the titles of unpublished works, including dissertations, lectures, and speeches.

10. Use arabic numerals except with names of monarchs (Elizabeth II) and except for the preliminary pages of a work (ii–xix), which traditionally use roman numerals.

11. Use lowercase abbreviations to identify the parts of a work (for example, *vol.* for *volume*), a named translator (*trans.*), and a named editor (*ed.*). However, when these designations follow a period, they should be capitalized (for example, Woolf, Virginia. A Writer's Diary. Ed. Leonard Woolf).

12. Whenever possible, use appropriate shortened forms for the publisher's name (*Random* instead of *Random House*). See the list of abbreviations beginning on page 58.

13. Separate author, title, and publication information with a period followed by one space.

14. Use a colon and one space to separate the volume number and year of a periodical from the page numbers (for example, Trimmer, Joseph. "Memoryscape: Jean Shepherd's Midwest." Old Northwest 2 (1976): 357–69).

In addition, MLA recommends procedures for documenting an extensive variety of sources, including nonprint materials such as films, television programs, and computer software. The following models illustrate the sources most commonly cited.

Books

When citing books, provide the following general categories of information:

Author's last name, first name. Book title. Additional

information. City of publication: Publishing company,

publication date.

Entries illustrating variations on this basic format appear below and are numbered to facilitate reference.

A Book by One Author

1. Boorstin, Daniel J. The Creators: A History of the

Heroes of the Imagination. New York: Random, 1992.

Two or More Books by the Same Author

2. Garreau, Joel. Edge City: Life on the New Frontier. New

York: Doubleday, 1991.

3. – – –. The Nine Nations of North America. Boston:

Houghton, 1981.

A Book by Two or Three Authors

4. Vare, Ethlie Ann, and Greg Ptacek. <u>Mothers of Invention: From the Bra to the Bomb: Forgotten Women and Their Unforgettable Ideas</u>. New York: Morrow, 1988.

5. Atwan, Robert, Donald McQuade, and John W. Wright. <u>Edsels, Luckies, and Frigidaires: Advertising the American Way</u>. New York: Dell, 1979.

A Book by Four or More Authors

6. Belenky, Mary Field, et al. <u>Women's Ways of Knowing: The Development of Self, Voice, and Mind</u>. New York: Basic, 1986.

A Book by a Corporate Author

7. Boston Women's Health Book Collective. <u>Our Bodies, Ourselves: A Book by and for Women</u>. New York: Simon, 1973.

A Book by an Anonymous Author

8. <u>Literary Market Place: The Dictionary of American Book Publishing</u>. 1993 ed. New York: Bowker, 1992.

A Book with an Editor

9. Hall, Donald, ed. <u>The Oxford Book of American Literary Anecdotes</u>. New York: Oxford UP, 1981.

A Book with an Author and an Editor

10. Toomer, Jean. <u>Cane</u>. Ed. Darwin T. Turner. New York: Norton, 1988.

A Book with a Publisher's Imprint

11. Kozol, Jonathan. <u>Illiterate America</u>. New York: Anchor-Doubleday, 1985.

An Anthology or Compilation

12. Valdez, Luis, and Stan Steiner, eds. <u>Aztlan: An Anthology of Mexican American Literature</u>. New York: Vintage-Knopf, 1972.

A Work in an Anthology

13. Silko, Leslie Marmon. "The Man to Send Rain Clouds." <u>Imagining America: Stories from the Promised Land</u>. Ed. Wesley Brown and Amy Ling. New York: Persea, 1991. 191–95.

An Introduction, Preface, Foreword, or Afterword

14. Bernstein, Carl. Afterword. <u>Poison Penmanship: The Gentle Art of Muckraking</u>. By Jessica Mitford. New York: Vintage-Random, 1979. 275–77.

A Multivolume Work

15. Blotner, Joseph. <u>Faulkner: A Biography</u>. 2 vols. New York: Random, 1974.

An Edition Other Than the First

16. Chaucer, Geoffrey. The Riverside Chaucer. Ed. Larry

    D. Benson. 3rd ed. Boston: Houghton, 1987.

A Book in a Series

17. McClave, Heather, ed. Women Writers of the Short

    Story. Twentieth Century Views. Englewood Cliffs,

    N.J.: Spectrum-Prentice, 1980.

A Republished Book

18. Malamud, Bernard. The Natural. 1952. New York:

    Avon, 1980.

A Signed Article in a Reference Book

19. Tobias, Richard. "Thurber, James." Encyclopedia

    Americana. 1991 ed.

An Unsigned Article in a Reference Book

20. "Tharp, Twyla." Who's Who of American Women. 17th

    ed. 1991–92.

A Government Document

21. United States. Cong. House. Committee on the

    Judiciary. Immigration and Nationality Act with

    Amendments and Notes on Related Laws. 7th ed.

    Washington: GPO, 1980.

Published Proceedings of a Conference

22. Griggs, John, ed. AIDS: Public Policy Dimensions.

    Proc. of a conference. 16–17 Jan. 1986. New York:

    United Hospital Fund of New York, 1987.

A Translation

23. Giroud, Françoise. Marie Curie: A Life. Trans. Lydia

    Davis. New York: Holmes, 1986.

A Book with a Title in Its Title

24. Habich, Robert D. Transcendentalism and the Western

    Messenger: A History of the Magazine and Its

    Contributors, 1835–1841. Rutherford, N.J.: Fairleigh

    Dickinson UP, 1985.

A Book Published before 1900

25. Field, Kate. The History of Bell's Telephone. London,

    1878.

An Unpublished Dissertation

26. Geissinger, Shirley Burry. "Openness versus Secrecy

    in Adoptive Parenthood." Diss. U of North Carolina at

    Greensboro, 1984.

A Published Dissertation

27. Ames, Barbara Edwards. <u>Dreams and Painting: A
    Case Study of the Relationship between an Artist's
    Dreams and Painting</u>. Diss. U of Virginia, 1978. Ann
    Arbor, Mich.: UMI, 1979. 7928021.

Articles in Periodicals

When citing articles in periodicals, provide the following general categories of information:

> Author's last name, first name. "Article title." <u>Periodical
> title</u> Date: inclusive pages.

Entries illustrating variations on this basic format appear below and are numbered to facilitate reference.

A Signed Article from a Daily Newspaper

28. Barringer, Felicity. "Where Many Elderly Live, Signs
    of the Future." <u>New York Times</u> 7 Mar. 1993, nat. ed.,
    sec. 1: 12.

An Unsigned Article from a Daily Newspaper

29. "Infant Mortality Down; Race Disparity Widens."
    <u>Washington Post</u> 12 Mar. 1993: A12.

An Article from a Monthly or Bimonthly Magazine

30. Wills, Garry. "The Words That Remade America:
    Lincoln at Gettysburg." <u>Atlantic</u> June 1992: 57–79.

An Article from a Weekly or Biweekly Magazine

31. Trillin, Calvin. "Culture Shopping." New Yorker 15
    Feb. 1993: 48–51.

An Article in a Journal with Continuous Pagination

32. Elbow, Peter. "Ranking, Evaluating, and Linking:
    Sorting Out Three Forms of Judgment." College
    English 55 (1993): 187–206.

An Article in a Journal That Numbers Each Issue Separately

33. Seely, Bruce. "The Saga of American Infrastructure: A
    Republic Bound Together." Wilson Quarterly 17.1
    (1993): 19–39.

An Editorial

34. "A Question of Medical Sight." Editorial. Plain Dealer
    [Cleveland, Ohio] 11 Mar. 1993: 6B.

A Review

35. Morson, Gary Soul. "Coping with Utopia." Rev. of
    Cultural History, by Andrei Sinyavsky. American
    Scholar 61 (1992): 132–38.

An Article Whose Title Contains a Quotation or a Title within Quotation Marks

36. DeCuir, André L. "Italy, England and the Female
    Artist in George Eliot's 'Mr. Gilfil's Love-Story.'"
    Studies in Short Fiction 29 (1992): 67–75.

An Abstract from *Dissertation Abstracts* or *Dissertation Abstracts International*

37. Creek, Mardena Bridges. "Myth, Wound,

Accommodation: American Literary Responses to the

War in Vietnam." DAI 43 (1982): 3539A. Ball State U.

CD-ROMs, Online Databases, and Computer Networks

When citing information from CD-ROMs, online databases, and computer networks, provide the following general categories of information:

Author's last name, first name. Publication for printed

source or printed analogue (i.e., "Article title."

Periodical title Date: inclusive pages). Title of

database. Publication medium (i.e., CD-ROM, online

database). Name of vendor or computer service.

Electronic publication date or date of access.

Entries illustrating variations on this basic format appear below and are numbered to facilitate reference.

CD-ROM: Printed Source or Printed Analogue

38. West, Cornel. "The Dilemma of the Black Intellectual."

Critical Quarterly 29 (1987): 39–52. MLA

International Bibliography. CD-ROM. SilverPlatter.

Feb. 1995.

CD-ROM: No Printed Source or Printed Analogue

39. PEPSICO Inc. "Company Profile." 3 October 1995.

Compact Disclosure. CD-ROM. Disclosure Inc. 10

March 1995.

CD-ROM: Nonperiodical Publication

40. Cinemania. CD-ROM. Redmond, Wash.: Microsoft,

1995.

CD-ROM: A Work in More Than One Medium

41. Mozart. CD-ROM. Laser optical disk. Union City, Calif.:

Ebook, 1992.

Online Database: Printed Source or Printed Analogue

42. Garfield, Donald. "Warhol's Starship Enterprise."

Museum News May/June 1994: 44–67. Art Index.

Online. OCLC First Search. 6 May 1995.

Online Database: No Printed Source or Printed Analogue

43. "Recycling Methods." Academic American

Encyclopedia. Online. Compuserve. 7 May 1995.

Computer Network: Electronic Journals, Newsletters, Conferences

44. Schreibman, Vigdor. "Closing the 'Values Gap.'" FINS

1.5 (8 March 1993): n.pag. Online. Internet. 10 April

1995.

Computer Network: Electronic Text

45. Stratton-Porter, Gene. Freckles. New York: Grosset,
    1904. Online. Wiretap. Internet. 1 May 1995.

Computer Network: Electronic Mail, Electronic Online Services

46. Penning, Sarah. "Mentor Advice." E-mail to Rai
    Peterson. 6 May 1995.

47. Pierson, Michael. "Internet Freedom." 30 April 1995.
    Online posting: alt.culture. Internet. Usenet. 3 May
    1995.

Other Sources

Films; Radio and Television Programs

48. The Last Emperor. Dir. Bernardo Bertolucci. With
    John Lone and Peter O'Toole. Columbia, 1987.

49. "If God Ever Listened: A Portrait of Alice Walker."
    Horizons. Prod. Jane Rosenthal. NPR. WBST, Muncie,
    Ind. 3 Mar. 1984.

50. "The Hero's Adventure." Moyers: Joseph Campbell
    and the Power of Myth. Prod. Catherine Tatge. PBS.
    WNET, New York. 23 May 1988.

Performances

51. A Walk in the Woods. By Lee Blessing. Dir. Des
    McAnuff. With Sam Waterston and Robert Prosky.
    Booth Theatre, New York. 17 May 1988.

52. Ozawa, Seiji, cond. Boston Symphony Orch. Concert.

Symphony Hall, Boston. 30 Sept. 1988.

Recordings

53. Mozart, Wolfgang A. Cosi Fan Tutte. Record. With Kiri

Te Kanawa, Frederica von Stade, David Rendall, and

Philippe Huttenlocher. Cond. Alain Lombard.

Strasbourg Philharmonic Orch. RCA, SRL3-2629,

1978.

54. Simon, Paul. "Under African Skies." Graceland.

Audiotape. Warner, 4-25447, 1980.

Works of Art

55. Botticelli, Sandro. Giuliano de' Medici. Samuel H.

Kress Collection. National Gallery of Art, Washington.

56. Rodin, Auguste. The Gate of Hell. Rodin Museum,

Paris.

Maps and Charts

57. Sonoma and Napa Counties. Map. San Francisco:

California State Automobile Assn., 1984.

Cartoons and Advertisements

58. Addams, Charles. Cartoon. New Yorker 22 Feb. 1988:

33.

59. Air France. "The Fine Art of Flying." Advertisement.

Travel and Leisure May 1988: 9.

Published and Unpublished Letters

60. Fitzgerald, F. Scott. "To Ernest Hemingway." 1 June
    1934. The Letters of F. Scott Fitzgerald. Ed. Andrew
    Turnbull. New York: Scribner's, 1963. 308–10.

61. Stowe, Harriet Beecher. Letter to George Eliot. 25 May
    1869. Berg Collection. New York: New York Public
    Library.

Interviews

62. Ellison, Ralph. "Indivisible Man." Interview. By James
    Alan McPherson. Atlantic Dec. 1970: 45–60.

63. Diamond, Carol. Telephone interview. 27 Dec. 1988.

Lectures, Speeches, and Addresses

64. Russo, Michael. "A Painter Speaks His Mind." Museum
    of Fine Arts. Boston, 5 Aug. 1984.

65. Baker, Houston A., Jr. "The Presidential Address."
    MLA Convention. New York, 28 Dec. 1992.

2. Documenting Sources

The purpose of a parenthetical reference is to document a source briefly, clearly, and accurately. Brevity can be accomplished in three ways.

1. Cite the author's last name and the page number(s) of the source in parentheses.

> One historian argues that since the invention of television "our politics, religion, news, athletics, education and commerce have been transformed into congenial adjuncts of show business, largely without protest or even much popular notice" (Postman 3–4).

2. Use the author's last name in your sentence, and place only the page number(s) of the source in parentheses.

> Postman points out that since the invention of television "our politics, religion, news, athletics, education and commerce have been transformed into congenial adjuncts of show business, largely without protest or even much popular notice" (3–4).

3. Give the author's last name in your sentence when you are citing the *entire* work rather than a *specific* section or passage, and omit any parenthetical reference.

> Postman argues that television has changed virtually
> every aspect of our culture into a form of show business.

Each of those textual references is brief and clear and refers readers to a specific and complete citation listed in Works Cited. The citation looks like this:

> Works Cited
>
> Postman, Neil. <u>Amusing Ourselves to Death: Public</u>
> <u>Discourse in the Age of Show Business</u>. New York:
> Penguin-Viking, 1985.

Placing and Punctuating the Parenthetical Reference

To avoid clutter in sentences, MLA recommends placing the parenthetical reference at the end of the sentence but before the final period. Notice that there is no punctuation mark between the author's name and the page citation.

> In the nineteenth century, the supposed golden age of
> American education, "college faculties acted as disciplinary
> tribunals, periodically reviewing violations of rules . . ."
> (Graff 25).

On some occasions, you may want to place the reference within your sentence to clarify its relationship to the part of the sentence it documents. In such instances, place the reference at the end of the clause but before the necessary comma.

> Graff suggests that even though college faculties in
>
> the nineteenth century "acted as disciplinary tribunals,
>
> periodically reviewing violations of rules" (25), the myth
>
> persists that they taught in the golden age of American
>
> education.

When the reference documents a long quotation that is set off from the text, place it at the end of the passage but *after* the final period.

> Gerald Graff's description of the college in the
>
> nineteenth century corrects the popular myth about the
>
> golden age of American education:
>
> > College faculties acted as disciplinary tribunals,
> >
> > periodically reviewing violations of rules such as
> >
> > those requiring students to attend chapel services
> >
> > early every morning, to remain in their rooms for
> >
> > hours every day, and to avoid the snares of town. Nor
> >
> > were these restrictions relaxed for the many students
> >
> > in their late twenties or older, who lived alongside
> >
> > freshmen as young as fourteen. The classes
> >
> > themselves, conducted by the system of daily
> >
> > recitations, were said to have "the fearsome
> >
> > atmosphere of a police-station." (25)

Works Cited

Graff, Gerald. <u>Professing Literature: An Institutional</u>
<u>History</u>. Chicago: U of Chicago P, 1987.

Citing Sources

Frequently, you will need to cite sources that are not as straight-forward as the examples given above. In those cases, you will need to modify the standard format according to the variations illustrated below. Each example is followed by the appropriate entry that would appear in the list of works cited.

1. Citing one work by the author of two or more works

If your list contains two or more titles by the same author, place a comma after the author's last name, add a shortened version of the title of the work, and then supply the relevant page numbers. Another solution is to cite the author's last name and title in your sentence and then add the page numbers in parentheses.

> Once society reaches a certain stage of industrial
> growth, it will shift its energies to the production of
> services (Toffler, <u>Future</u> 221).
> Toffler argues in <u>The Third Wave</u> that society has
> gone through two eras (agricultural and industrial) and is
> now entering another--the information age (26).

Works Cited

Toffler, Alvin. <u>Future Shock</u>. New York: Random, 1970.

– – –. <u>The Third Wave</u>. New York: Morrow, 1980.

2. Citing one work by an author who has the same last name as another author in your list

When your list contains sources by two or more authors with the same last name, avoid confusion by adding the initial of the author's first name in the parenthetical reference and the author's first name in your sentence. In the list of works cited, the two authors should be alphabetized according to first name.

> Critics have often debated the usefulness of the psychological approach to literary interpretation (F. Hoffman 317).
>
> Daniel Hoffman argues that folklore and myth provide valuable insights for the literary critic (9–10).

Works Cited

Hoffman, Daniel G. Form and Fable in American Fiction.

New York: Oxford UP, 1961.

Hoffman, Frederick J. Freudianism and the Literary

Mind. Baton Rouge: Louisiana State UP, 1945.

3. Citing a multivolume work

If you are citing one volume of a multivolume work, indicate in your parenthetical reference the specific volume you used.

> William Faulkner's initial reluctance to travel to Stockholm to receive the Nobel Prize produced considerable consternation in the American embassy (Blotner 2: 1347).

Works Cited

Blotner, Joseph. Faulkner: A Biography. 2 vols. New York:

Random, 1974.

4. Citing a work by more than one author

If you are citing a book by two or three authors, you may supply their last names in a parenthetical reference or in your sentence. To sustain the readability of your sentence if you are citing a book by four or more authors, use the first author's last name and *et al.* ("and others") in a parenthetical reference or in your sentence.

> Boller and Story interpret the Declaration of
> Independence as Thomas Jefferson's attempt to list
> America's grievances against England (2: 62).
>
> Other historians view the Declaration of
> Independence as Jefferson's attempt to formulate the
> principles of America's political philosophy (Norton
> et al. 141).

> Works Cited
>
> Boller, Paul F., Jr., and Ronald Story. <u>A More Perfect</u>
> <u>Union: Documents in U.S. History</u>. 2 vols. 3rd ed.
> Boston: Houghton, 1992.
>
> Norton, Mary Beth, et al. <u>A People and a Nation: A</u>
> <u>History of the United States</u>. 4th ed. Boston:
> Houghton, 1994.

5. Citing a work by title

In the list of works cited, alphabetize works by anonymous authors according to the first main word in the title. The initial articles *a, an,* and *the* are not counted as first words. A shortened version of the title—or the title itself, if it is short—replaces the author's last name in the text citation or parenthetical reference.

If you shorten the title, be sure to begin with the word under which the source is alphabetized in the list of works cited.

> The recent exhibit of nineteenth-century patent
>
> models at the Cooper-Hewitt Museum featured plans for
>
> such inventions as the Rotating Blast-Producing Chair, an
>
> Improved Creeping-Doll, and the Life-Preserving Coffin: In
>
> Doubtful Cases of Actual Death ("Talk").

Notice that this example follows MLA's recommendation to omit page numbers in a parenthetical reference when citing a one-page article.

> Works Cited
>
> "The Talk of the Town." New Yorker. 16 July 1984: 23.

6. Citing a work by a corporate author or government agency

If the author of your source is a corporation or a government agency, you may include the appropriate citation in parentheses (American Telephone and Telegraph 3). It is more graceful, however, to include this information in your sentence, particularly if you are citing several corporate or government reports in one text.

> American Telephone and Telegraph's Annual Report
>
> for 1982 announced that the corporation had reached a
>
> turning point in its history (3).
>
> Works Cited
>
> American Telephone and Telegraph. Annual Report 1982.
>
> New York: American Telephone and Telegraph, 1983.

7. Citing literary works

Because literary works—novels, plays, poems—are available in many editions, MLA recommends that you provide information in addition to page numbers, so that readers using different editions can locate the passage you are citing. After the page number, add a semicolon and other appropriate information, using lowercase abbreviations such as *pt., sec., ch.*

> Although Flaubert sees Madame Bovary for what she is - - a silly, romantic woman - - he insists that "none of us can ever express the exact measure of his needs or his thoughts or his sorrows" and that all of us "long to make music that will melt the stars" (216; pt. 2, ch. 12).
>
> Works Cited
>
> Flaubert, Gustave. Madame Bovary: Patterns of Provincial Life. Trans. Francis Steegmuller. New York: Modern Library–Random, 1957.

When citing classic verse plays and poems, omit all page numbers and document by division(s) and line(s), using periods to separate the various numbers. You can also use appropriate abbreviations to designate certain well-known works. For example, *Od.* 8.326 refers to book 8, line 326, of Homer's *Odyssey.* Do not use the abbreviation *l.* or *ll.* to indicate lines because the letters can be confused with numbers.

Also, as shown in the *Odyssey* citation above, use arabic rather than roman numerals to indicate divisions and page numbers. Some teachers still prefer to use roman numerals for documenting acts and scenes in plays (for example, *Macbeth* III.iv). If your instructor does not insist on this practice, follow MLA style and use arabic numerals (and appropriate abbreviations) to cite famous plays — *Mac.* 3.4.

8. Citing more than one work in a single parenthetical reference

If you need to include two or more works in a single reference, document each reference according to the normal pattern, but separate each citation with a semicolon.

(Oleson 59; Trimble 85; Hylton 63)

Works Cited

Hylton, Marion Willard. "On a Trail of Pollen: Momaday's

House Made of Dawn." Critique: Studies in Modern

Fiction 14.2 (1972): 60–69.

Oleson, Carole. "The Remembered Earth: Momaday's

House Made of Dawn." South Dakota Review 11

(1973): 59–78.

Trimble, Martha Scott. N. Scott Momaday. Boise State

College Western Writers Series. Boise, Idaho: Boise

State Col., 1973.

Although MLA style provides this procedure for documenting multiple citations in one parenthetical reference, MLA recommends citing multiple sources in a numbered bibliographic note rather than parenthetically in the text.

3. Using Notes and Parenthetical References

In MLA style, notes (preferably endnotes) are reserved for two specific purposes.

1. **To supply additional commentary on the information in the text**

> Thurber's reputation continued to grow until the 1950s, when he was forced to give up drawing because of his blindness.[1]

> Note
>
> [1] Thurber's older brother accidentally shot him in the eye with an arrow when they were children, causing the immediate loss of that eye. He gradually lost the sight of the other eye because of complications from the accident and a cataract.

2. **To list (and perhaps evaluate) several sources or to refer readers to additional sources**

> The argument that American policy in Vietnam was on the whole morally justified has come under attack from many quarters.[1]

Note

¹ For a useful sampling of opinion, see Draper 32

and Nardin and Slater 437.

Notice that the sources cited in this note are documented like parenthetical references and the note itself directs readers to the complete citation in the list of works cited.

Works Cited

Draper, Theodore. "Ghosts of Vietnam." Dissent 26

(1979): 30–41.

Nardin, Terry, and Jerome Slater. "Vietnam Revisited."

World Politics 33 (1981): 436–48.

As illustrated above, a note is signaled with a superscript numeral (a number raised above the line) typed at an appropriate place in the text (most often at the end of a sentence). The note itself, identified by a matching number followed by a space, appears at the end of the text (an endnote) or at the bottom of the page (a footnote). MLA recommends that you keep such notes to a minimum so that readers are not distracted from your main point.

4. Implications for Your Research and Writing

MLA style emphasizes the importance of following the procedures for planning and writing a research paper outlined in any standard writing textbook. In particular, MLA style requires you to devote considerable attention to certain steps in your research and composing.

Compiling Source Cards

Once you have located sources that you suspect will prove useful, fill out a source card for each item. List the source in the appropriate format (use the formats shown in the guidelines for preparing the list of works cited, pages 5–18). To guarantee that each card is complete and accurate, take your information directly from the source rather than from a card catalogue or a bibliographical index. Your collection of cards will help you keep track of your sources throughout your research. Alphabetizing the cards will enable you to prepare a provisional list of works cited.

The provisional list must be in place *before* you begin writing your paper. You may expand or refine the list as you write, but to document each source in your text, you first need to know its correct citation. Thus, although Works Cited will be the last section of your paper, you must prepare it first.

Writing Note Cards

Taking notes demands that you read, select, interpret, and evaluate the information that will form the substance of your paper. After you return books and articles to the library, your notes will be the only record of your research. If you have taken notes carelessly, you will be in trouble when you try to use them in your paper. Many students inadvertently plagiarize because they are working from inaccurate note cards. As you select information from a source, use one of three methods to record it on an individual note card: quoting, summarizing, or paraphrasing.

Quoting Sources

Although quoting an author's text word for word is the easiest way to record information, use this method selectively and quote only the passages that deal directly with your subject in memorable language. When you copy a quotation onto a note card, place quotation marks at the beginning and the end of the passage. If you decide to omit part of the passage, use ellipsis points to indicate that you have omitted words from the original source. To indicate an omission from the middle of a sentence, use ellipses (. . .) and leave a space before and after each period. For an omission at the end of a sentence, use ellipses following the sentence period.

To make a quotation fit smoothly into the flow of your text, use one of the following methods.

1. Work the quoted passage into the syntax of your sentence.

Morrison points out that social context prevented the authors of slave narratives "from dwelling too long or too carefully on the more sordid details of their experience" (109).

2. Introduce the quoted passage with a sentence and a colon.

Commentators have tried to account for the decorum of most slave narratives by discussing social context: "popular taste discouraged the writers from dwelling too long or too carefully on the more sordid details of their experience" (Morrison 109).

3. Set off the quoted passage with an introductory sentence followed by a colon.

This method is reserved for long quotations (four or more lines of prose; three or more lines of poetry). Double-space the quotation, and indent it ten spaces or one inch from the left margin. Because this special placement identifies the passage as a quotation, do not enclose it within quotation marks. Notice that the final period goes *before* rather than *after* the parenthetical reference. Leave one space after the final period.

Toni Morrison, in "The Site of Memory," explains how social context shaped slave narratives:

. . . no slave society in the history of the world wrote more--or more thoughtfully--about its own

enslavement. The milieu, however, dictated the
purpose and the style. The narratives are instructive,
moral and obviously representative. Some of them
are patterned after the sentimental novel that was in
vogue at the time. But whatever the level of
eloquence or the form, popular taste discouraged the
writers from dwelling too long or too carefully on the
more sordid details of their experience. (109)

Summarizing and Paraphrasing Sources

Summarizing and paraphrasing an author's text are the most
efficient ways to record information. The terms *summary* and
paraphrase are often used interchangeably to describe a brief
restatement of the author's ideas in your own words, but they
may be used more precisely to designate different procedures. A
summary condenses the content of a lengthy passage. When you
write a summary, you reformulate the main idea and outline the
main points that support it. A *paraphrase* restates the content of
a short passage. When you write a paraphrase, you reconstruct
the passage phrase by phrase, recasting the author's words in
your own.

A summary or a paraphrase is intended as a complete and
objective presentation of an author's ideas, so do not distort the
original passage by omitting major points or by adding your own
opinion. Because the words of a summary or a paraphrase are
yours, they are not enclosed by quotation marks. But because
the ideas you are stating came from someone else, you need to
cite the source on your note card and in your text. (See "Avoiding
Plagiarism," page 35.)

The following examples illustrate two common methods of introducing a summary or a paraphrase into your paper.

1. Summary of a long quotation (see the Morrison quotation on pages 32–33)

Often, the best way to proceed is to name the author of a source in the body of your sentence and place the page numbers in parentheses. This procedure informs your reader that you are about to quote or paraphrase. It also gives you an opportunity to state the credentials of the authority you are citing.

> Award-winning novelist Toni Morrison argues that although slaves wrote many powerful narratives, the context of their enslavement prevented them from telling the whole truth about their lives (109).

2. Paraphrase of a short quotation (see the fourth sentence of the Morrison quotation)

You may decide to vary the pattern of documentation by presenting the information from a source and placing the author's name and page numbers in parentheses at the end of the sentence. This method is particularly useful if you have already established the identity of your source in a previous sentence and now want to develop the author's ideas in some detail without having to clutter your sentences with constant references to him or her.

> Slave narratives sometimes imitated the popular fiction of their era (Morrison 109).

Works Cited

Morrison, Toni. "The Site of Memory." Inventing the
Truth: The Art and Craft of Memoir. Ed. William
Zinsser. Boston: Houghton, 1987. 101–24.

Avoiding Plagiarism

Plagiarism is using someone else's words or ideas without giving proper credit—or without giving any credit at all—to the writer of the original. Whether plagiarism is intentional or unintentional, it is a serious offense that you can avoid by adhering to the advice for research and writing outlined above.

The following excerpt is from Robert Hughes's *The Fatal Shore*, an account of the founding of Australia. The examples of how students tried to use this excerpt illustrate the problem of plagiarism.

Original Version

Transportation did not stop crime in England or even
slow it down. The "criminal class" was not eliminated by
transportation, and could not be, because transportation
did not deal with the causes of crime.

Version A

Transportation did not stop crime in England or even
slow it down. Criminals were not eliminated by transportation because transportation did not deal with the
causes of crime.

Version A is plagiarism. Because the writer of Version A does not indicate in the text or in a parenthetical reference that the words and ideas belong to Hughes, her readers will believe the words are hers. She has stolen the words and ideas and has attempted to cover the theft by changing or omitting an occasional word.

Version B

> Robert Hughes points out that transportation did not stop crime in England or even slow it down. The criminal class was not eliminated by transportation, and could not be, because transportation did not deal with the causes of crime (168).

Version B is also plagiarism, even though the writer acknowledges his source and documents the passage with a parenthetical reference. He has worked from careless notes and has misunderstood the difference between quoting and paraphrasing. He has copied the original word for word yet has supplied no quotation marks to indicate the extent of the borrowing. As written and documented, the passage masquerades as a paraphrase when in fact it is a direct quotation.

Version C

> Hughes argues that transporting criminals from England to Australia "did not stop crime. . . . The 'criminal class' was not eliminated by transportation, and could not be, because transportation did not deal with the causes of crime" (168).

Version C is one satisfactory way of handling this source material. The writer has identified her source at the beginning of the sentence, letting readers know who is being quoted. She then explains the concept of transportation in her own words, placing within quotation marks the parts of the original she wants to quote and using ellipses to delete the parts she wants to omit. She provides a parenthetical reference to the page number in the source listed in Works Cited.

Works Cited

Hughes, Robert. <u>The Fatal Shore</u>. New York: Knopf, 1987.

5. Sample Outline and Research Paper

The author of the following research paper used many features of MLA style to document her paper. At her instructor's request, she first submitted a final version of her thesis and outline. Adhering to MLA style, she did not include a title page with her outline or her paper. Instead, she typed her name, her instructor's name, the course title, and the date on separate lines (double-spaced) at the upper left margin. Then, after double-spacing again, she typed the title of her paper, double-spaced, and started the first line of her text. On page 1 and successive pages, she typed her last name and the page number in the upper right-hand corner, as recommended by MLA.

Taraskiewicz 1

Jill Taraskiewicz

Mr. Johnson

English 104, Section 3

4 November 1992

The Recycling Controversy

Thesis: By examining both sides in the controversy, we

can understand how recycling fits into our environmental

policy.

I. Critics contend that recycling has become expensive.

   A. Recycling plants are not cost efficient.

   B. Recycling collection strains budgets.

   C. Recycling technology does not repay investment.

II. Critics argue that recycling is inefficient.

   A. Some materials are in over supply.

   B. Other materials are in short supply.

III. Critics suggest abandoning recycling.

   A. Landfills cost less.

   B. Incinerators seem more efficient.

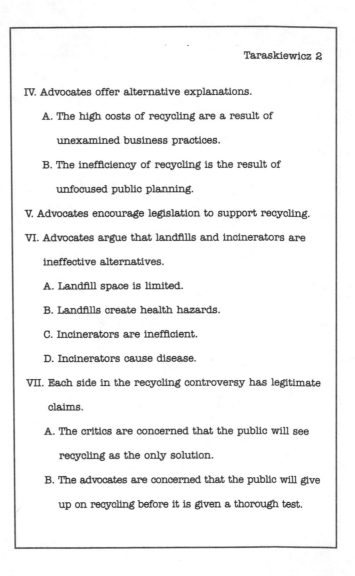

Taraskiewicz 2

IV. Advocates offer alternative explanations.

    A. The high costs of recycling are a result of unexamined business practices.

    B. The inefficiency of recycling is the result of unfocused public planning.

V. Advocates encourage legislation to support recycling.

VI. Advocates argue that landfills and incinerators are ineffective alternatives.

    A. Landfill space is limited.

    B. Landfills create health hazards.

    C. Incinerators are inefficient.

    D. Incinerators cause disease.

VII. Each side in the recycling controversy has legitimate claims.

    A. The critics are concerned that the public will see recycling as the only solution.

    B. The advocates are concerned that the public will give up on recycling before it is given a thorough test.

Taraskiewicz 3

VIII. Recycling has a limited role in our environmental

policy.

A. Not all forms of recycling are equal.

B. No single process such as recycling will solve our

complex garbage problem.

C. In addition to waste management, we need to

practice waste reduction.

Double-space

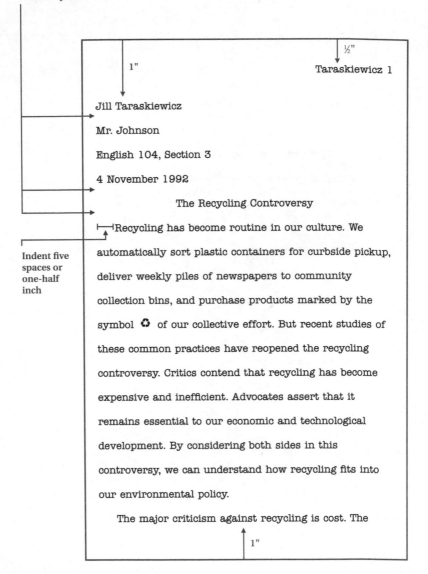

½"

Taraskiewicz 1

1"

Jill Taraskiewicz

Mr. Johnson

English 104, Section 3

4 November 1992

The Recycling Controversy

Recycling has become routine in our culture. We

Indent five
spaces or
one-half
inch

automatically sort plastic containers for curbside pickup,

deliver weekly piles of newspapers to community

collection bins, and purchase products marked by the

symbol ♻ of our collective effort. But recent studies of

these common practices have reopened the recycling

controversy. Critics contend that recycling has become

expensive and inefficient. Advocates assert that it

remains essential to our economic and technological

development. By considering both sides in this

controversy, we can understand how recycling fits into

our environmental policy.

The major criticism against recycling is cost. The

1"

Paraphrase: Author and page
number are placed in parentheses.

Taraskiewicz 2

simple process of sorting plastic containers for curbside

pickup does not anticipate the expense of collecting,

separating, and reprocessing the seven basic types of

plastic at the recycling plant (Van Voorst 53). Indeed,

those procedures do not approach cost effectiveness until

plants can collect enough raw material to keep the

recycling machines running continuously. John Bell

reports in the New Scientist that "Germany gave up

the idea of trying to run a recycling plant at Coburg

because it could not find 5 tons of waste plastic a day

within 100 kilometers" (44). Even consumer advocate

Lynn Scarlett acknowledges that putting one set of trucks

on the road "to pick up recyclables, [and] another for

remaining waste" not only strains community budgets but

also creates more fuel consumption and air pollution.

The cost of recycling is dramatically evident in the

elaborate "de-inking" technology required to convert old

newspapers into reusable paper. In his study, Dan

Short quotation: Author and source are identified in
sentence; page number is placed in parentheses.

Long quotation: A quotation of more than four typed lines is indented ten spaces or one inch and does not require quotation marks.

Taraskiewicz 3

Charles describes some of the complicated steps in this

expensive procedure:

> The process relies on turning old paper into pulp
>
> with water and chemicals, before spinning it in
>
> tubes to remove any heavy contaminants like
>
> staples or sand. . . . Ink particles attach
>
> themselves to air bubbles and rise to the surface,
>
> where they are scraped off. . . . [T]he paper fibers
>
> are bleached with hydrogen peroxide. . . . None of
>
> these processes do very well at removing or
>
> hiding laser print, glue or paper coatings. (13)

Because of the cost of such procedures - - $50 million to

build one plant - - many newsprint producers are

reluctant to invest in deinking technology. Marcia Berss

points out that recycling newspapers does not really

save trees: "U.S. virgin newsprint is largely made from

trees grown as a crop" (41). This agro-business has

created such an "overcapacity of virgin newsprint" that

Short quotation: The quotation is introduced with an independent clause and set off by a colon.

Taraskiewicz 4

newsprint producers see "no way to recoup the cost of capital outlays" for recycling plants (Berss 41).

Although recent studies of recycling discuss cost, they are more concerned about efficiency. The real issues, they contend, are the inequities in supply and demand. Old newspapers are in great supply. "New Jersey towns that just nine months ago pulled in $20 a ton for newsprint must now pay up to $10 a ton to ship it away" (Cahan 116). Indeed, Bruce Van Voorst reveals that over 100 million tons of newspaper collected in the United States never get recycled (52). Moreover, the demand for recycled paper is so depressed that some states have had to pass legislation forcing newspapers to print part of each new edition on recycled paper (Yang 100H). By contrast, plastic is in short supply. Bell reports that although the world produces around 100 million tons of plastic a year, "not enough is reclaimed to enable the manufacturing industry to develop and

Short quotation: Author is identified at the beginning of the writer's sentence, and the quotation is worked into the remaining portion of the sentence.

Taraskiewicz 5

market products made of recycled material" (44).

Wellman, Inc., America's largest plastic recycler, "gobbled

up most of the 1.5 billion two liter bottles handed in for

recycling" but could supply only half of the demand for

its product (Cahan 116–17).

These studies have prompted some critics to conclude

that we should abandon recycling. Landfills cost less.

Berss points out that this year the citizens of San Jose,

California, "will spend $160 a ton to recycle their waste,

versus $93 a ton to dump it" (41). Incinerators seem

more efficient. Bell explains why plastics are useful for

the incineration of municipal waste: "If plastics

are removed from waste along with other flammable

solids such as paper, what is left is too wet to burn. But

if the waste is burned with the plastics still there,

potentially useful energy is generated" (44).

These same studies have prompted recycling

advocates to generate alternative explanations for the

Paraphrase: Author and source are identified at the beginning
of the sentence, referring to the interview in Works Cited.

Taraskiewicz 6

problems of cost and efficiency. Much of what appears as

excessive cost, they argue, is really the result of long-

established and unexamined business practices. Van

Voorst reports that the oil depletion allowance provides a

significant subsidy for the producers of oil-based

plastics (53). In an interview, environmentalist Pamela

Popovich points out that American railroads charge more

by the ton to haul recycled paper than they charge to

ship virgin paper. "If these costs are taken into

consideration," contends Allen Hershkowitz, senior

scientist at the Natural Resources Defense Council,

"recycling looks economically a lot more competitive"

(Van Voorst 53).

The inefficiencies in recycling, say advocates, are the

result of bad press, poor planning, and underdeveloped

technology. "Contrary to popular belief, recycled paper is

as high-quality as the conventional stuff and

competitively priced" (McAllister). Cahan indicates that

Short quotation: Ellipses are used in the middle of the quoted passage to shorten and focus the material.

Taraskiewicz 7

when "state officials from Rhode Island, New York, and other Northeastern states met with the region's newspaper publishers and paper industry groups to push for the increased use of recycled paper," they seemed to get good results (117). Recyclers would get even better results with more effective technology. As Van Voorst suggests, "new processes . . . are needed to remove contaminants. Sorted solid wastes often include contaminants that gum up recycling systems, such as clear plastic tape on envelopes or sticky yellow Post-its on office paper" (54).

The most direct method for cutting costs and increasing efficiency is legislation. Charles reports that "every one of the 50 states in the U.S. has now passed a law that either encourages or requires local governments to set up some kind of recycling program" (12). Some laws require citizens to sort "each kind of rubbish in its own distinctive container" (Charles 12). Others mandate

Documentation: Both quotation and paraphrase are documented by author and page in parentheses.

Summary: Lengthy arguments are summarized;
authors and page numbers are placed in parentheses.

Taraskiewicz 8

the minimum use of recycled materials in new products

(Berss 41). Still others use tax incentives to encourage

companies to develop new technologies (Van Voorst 52).

Recycling advocates are willing to support such

extensive legislation because they are adamantly

opposed to the alternatives--landfills and incinerators.

Landfills may be inexpensive and convenient, but space

is limited and continues to decline (Glenn and Riggle 35).

Where space is still available--in poor and sparsely

populated areas--citizens are concerned about whether

the deposit income justifies the dumping of garbage from

rich communities out of state. Nobody wants to live next

to a landfill, particularly when it can contaminate air,

soil, and water (Gialanella and Luedtke SW/RR 18).

Incinerators may cost less than recycling, but they

are hardly efficient. Nancy Shute reports that "even if all

[of New York's] five incinerators are up and running at

full tilt, they could only burn 12,000 tons of garbage

Documentation: Parenthetical reference
reveals special page numbering in source.

Quotation: Authors and source are identified in an introductory phrase, and the quotation is worked into the rest of the sentence.

Taraskiewicz 9

a day, less than half the amount the city now creates"
(48). More important, incinerators create serious air
pollution. In a letter to the New York Times, Elizabeth
Holtzman indicates that "lead and mercury are emitted
from garbage incinerators in large quantities, and can
cause brain damage in children." And according to
William Rathje and Cullen Murphy, authors of Rubbish!
The Archaeology of Garbage, even "well run incinerators
can release into the atmosphere small amounts of more
than twenty-five metals . . . which have been implicated
in birth defects and several kinds of cancer" (180).

Recycling is controversial because both sides present
legitimate arguments. The critics are concerned that the
public will see recycling as the solution to the complex
problem of resource management. There is simply too
much garbage and too little technology to justify this
solution. Even in those instances where economies and
technology may justify recycling, the critics are

Summary: Complex information is summarized in the writer's own words and documented with a parenthetical reference.

Taraskiewicz 10

concerned that the procedures may create unac-

knowledged environmental problems such as high

volumes of water waste and energy consumption

(Scarlett).

The advocates are concerned that the public will give

up on recycling before improvements in education,

technology, and public policy explore its potential as a

solution to resource management. As Rathje and Murphy

point out, "recycling is a fragile and complicated piece of

economic and social machinery--a space shuttle rather

than a tractor; it may frequently break down" (239). But

advocates are willing to invest in the eventual success of

recycling, particularly when they consider alternatives

such as landfills and incinerators.

Although critics and advocates make legitimate

claims, we need a larger perspective to understand the

place of recycling in our environmental policy. First, we

must realize that all types of recycling are not equal.

**Long quotation: Major evidence to support the
writer's thesis is highlighted by a block quotation.**

Taraskiewicz 11

John E. Young explains how to sort out the different

types:

> The most valuable is the manufacture of new
>
> products from similar, used items; the least
>
> valuable is the conversion of waste materials into
>
> entirely different products. The key criterion is
>
> whether the recovered material is substituted for
>
> the virgin one in production, thus closing the
>
> loop. (27)

Some materials--such as glass, steel, and aluminum--

rank high in this scheme because they save virgin

material from being used. Some--such as plastic--rank

low because virtually none is "now being recycled back

into original containers" (Young 27). Still others--such

as paper--fall somewhere in between because "each

time paper is recycled, the fibers it contains are

shortened by the process, making the new paper

weaker" (Young 27).

Quotation: Quoted material is marked with double quotation marks; quotations *within* the quotation are marked with single quotation marks.

Taraskiewicz 12

Second, we must become what Rathje and Murphy

call "garbage literate" because the label ♻ that

identifies products as recycled can be deceptive (242). In

most cases, manufacturers use the recycling symbol to

indicate that their products are environmentally friendly

and responsible. But these products are rarely made

from materials that have been turned in for recycling.

Instead, they are made from "pre-consumer" waste--

that is, material left over from the manufacturing

process. Rathje and Murphy point out that the "label one

needs to look for is 'post-consumer recycled,' and ideally

the label will include a percentage, as in '30 percent

post-consumer recycled.' Anything over 10 percent is

worthwhile" (243).

Third, we must acknowledge that our garbage

problem is so complex that no one process--such as

recycling--will ever provide a single solution. Larry

Schaper argues that the nation will continue to need

Short quotation: Authors are identified in the writer's introductory clause; quotation is worked into the writer's sentence.

Taraskiewicz 13

landfills, and "as the industry gains more control over

the types of materials going into municipal landfills and

landfill designs become more reliable, the public may

become more accepting of landfills" (65). Similarly,

Gialanella and Luedtke argue that recent technological

advances in the design of incinerators have improved

"their ability to safeguard the environment and public

health" (SW/RR 32). Rathje and Murphy contend that

the goal is not to "bow" before one single approach but

"to discern the varying roles each of these approaches

should play locally in America's widely disparate

communities and regions" (239).

    Finally, we need to develop other environmental

policies such as waste reduction. Anne Magnuson reports

that some communities encourage their citizens to

precycle--that is, to buy products in bulk rather than in

many small containers that require recycling. Other

communities discourage the accumulation of waste by

Summary: Author is identified at the beginning of a series of
assertions about waste reduction that contribute to the writer's
conclusion. Documentation cites inclusive page numbers.

Taraskiewicz 14

charging a flat fee for every trash bag. And some
encourage citizens to use printed postcards to remove
their names from junk mailing lists (30–37). Such
policies discourage the introduction of more waste into
the system. Unless we develop such waste reduction
policies, all the recycling, landfills, and incinerators in
the world will not save us from our own garbage.

Double-space

½"

1"   Taraskiewicz 15

Works Cited

Bell, John. "Plastics: Waste Not, Want Not." New Scientist

Indent five
spaces or
one-half
inch

1 Dec. 1990: 44–47.

Berss, Marcia. "Nobody Wants to Shoot Snow White."

Forbes 14 Oct. 1991: 40–42.

Cahan, Vicky. "Waste Not, Want Not? Not Necessarily."

Business Week 17 July 1989: 116–17.

An article
in a weekly
magazine.

Charles, Dan. "Too Many Bottles Break the Bank." New

Scientist 18 (Apr. 1992): 12–13.

Gialanella, Mario, and Louis Luedtke. "Air Pollution

Control and Waste Management." American City and

County 106 (Jan. 1991): SW/RR 17–32.

Glenn, Jim, and David Riggle. "The State of Garbage in

America." Bio Cycle 32 (Apr. 1991): 34–38.

Holtzman, Elizabeth. Letter. New York Times 24 Jan.

1992: A28.

Magnuson, Anne. "What Has Happened to Waste

Reduction?" American City and County 106 (Apr.

1991): 30–37.

The form for documenting a letter published
in a newspaper divided into sections.

An article by three authors.

Taraskiewicz 16

McAllister, Celia. "Save the Trees - - And You May Save a

Bundle." Business Week 4 Sept. 1989: 118.

Popovich, Pamela. Personal interview. 12 Oct. 1992.

Rathje, William, and Cullen Murphy. Rubbish! The

Archaeology of Garbage. New York: Harper, 1992.

Scarlett, Lynn. "Will Recycling Help the Environment?"

Consumer Research 74 (Mar. 1991): 17.

Schaper, Larry. "Trends in Landfill Planning and Design."

Public Works 122 (Apr. 1991): 64–65.

Shute, Nancy. "The Mound Builder." Amicus Journal 12

(Summer 1990): 44–49.

Van Voorst, Bruce. "The Recycling Bottleneck." Time 14

Sept. 1992: 52–54.

Yang, Dori Jones, William C. Symonds, and Lisa Driscoll.

"Recycling Is Rewriting the Rules in Papermaking."

Business Week 22 Apr. 1991: 100H–100L.

Young, John E. Discarding the Throwaway Society.

Washington: Worldwatch, 1991.

A book by one author.

6. Abbreviations for MLA Documentation

Selected Publishers

When the publisher's name is the name of one person (Harry N. Abrams, Inc.), cite the surname alone (Abrams). When the publisher's name uses the names of more than one person (Harcourt Brace), cite only the first of these names (Harcourt).

Abrams	Harry N. Abrams, Inc.
Allyn	Allyn and Bacon, Inc.
Appleton	Appleton-Century-Crofts
Basic	Basic Books
Bowker	R. R. Bowker Co.
Dodd	Dodd, Mead, and Co.
Doubleday	Doubleday and Co., Inc.
Farrar	Farrar, Straus, and Giroux, Inc.
Feminist	The Feminist Press at the City University of New York
Harcourt	Harcourt Brace
Harper	HarperCollins
Harvard UP	Harvard University Press
Holt	Holt, Rinehart and Winston, Inc.
Houghton	Houghton Mifflin Co.
Knopf	Alfred A. Knopf, Inc.
Lippincott	J. B. Lippincott Co.
MIT P	The MIT Press
MLA	The Modern Language Association of America
Norton	W. W. Norton and Co., Inc.
Oxford UP	Oxford University Press, Inc.
Princeton UP	Princeton University Press

Rand	Rand McNally and Co.
Random	Random House, Inc.
St. Martin's	St. Martin's Press, Inc.
Scribner's	Charles Scribner's Sons
Simon	Simon and Schuster, Inc.
UMI	University Microfilms International
U of Chicago P	University of Chicago Press
Viking	The Viking Press, Inc.
Yale UP	Yale University Press

Selected Reference Resources

BM	British Museum, London (now British Library)
Cong. Rec.	*Congressional Record*
DA, DAI	*Dissertation Abstracts, Dissertation Abstracts International*
DAB	*Dictionary of American Biography*
DNB	*Dictionary of National Biography*
ERIC—ED	Educational Resources Information Center— Educational Document
ERIC—EJ	Educational Resources Information Center— Educational Journal
GPO	Government Printing Office, Washington, D.C.
HMSO	Her (His) Majesty's Stationery Office
LC	Library of Congress
NPR	National Public Radio
PBS	Public Broadcasting System
PC–DOS	Personal Computer–Disk Operating System

Appendix on APA Style

The purpose of documentation is twofold: (1) to avoid representing somebody else's work as your own and (2) to refer readers to the specific source you are citing. Although there is general agreement about the purpose of documentation, different fields of knowledge use different styles. If you are writing a research paper in the humanities, your instructor is likely to require MLA style. If you are writing a research paper in the social sciences, your instructor is likely to require APA style, the style of the American Psychological Association.

In some ways, APA and MLA styles are similar. Both require an alphabetized list of sources and parenthetical documentation of citations in the text. Both use numbered notes only to convey certain kinds of information not included in the text. Some major differences between the two styles, especially APA's emphasis on date of publication, are reflected in the guidelines and illustrations given below. For further information, see the *Publication Manual of the American Psychological Association,* 4th ed. (Washington: APA, 1994).

Preparing the List of References

1. Paginate the list of sources (entitled **References**) as a continuation of your text.

2. Double-space successive lines of an entry and between entries.

3. Begin the first line of an entry flush left, and indent successive lines three spaces.

4. List the entries in alphabetical order according to the last name of the author.

5. If you are listing more than one work by the same author, arrange the works by date of publication, starting with the earliest work. Repeat the author's name in each entry.

6. Invert the names of all authors in each entry, and use initials for the first and middle names of all authors.

7. When there is more than one author, use an ampersand (&) before the name of the last author.

8. When there is more than one author, name all the authors in the list of references. (In the text, if there are more than six authors, list only the first author and use *et al.* for the rest.)

9. Place the date of publication in parentheses immediately after the author's name. Place a period after the closing parenthesis.

10. If you list two works by the same author published in the same year, arrange the works alphabetically by title (excluding the articles *a* and *the*) and assign letters to the year to prevent confusion—(1984a), (1984b).

11. Place the article title (if any) or book title after the year of publication.

12. In references to books, capitalize only the first word of the title, the first word of the subtitle (if any), and all proper names. Underline the complete book title.

13. If the author is also the publisher of the work, put the word *Author* after the place of publication.

14. In references to articles in periodicals or in edited volumes, capitalize only the first word of the title, the first word of the subtitle (if any), and all proper names. Do not enclose the title in quotation marks. Put a period after the title.

15. Spell out the names of journals in upper- and lowercase letters, and underline the journal name.

16. In references to periodicals, give the volume number in arabic numerals and underline it. Do not use *vol.* before the number.

17. Use *p.* or *pp.* for page numbers in references to newspapers and magazines. Omit *p.* or *pp.* in references to journal articles.

Sample Entries

When citing books and articles, provide the following general categories of information:

> Author's last name, first initial. (Publication date). Book
>
> title. Additional information. City of publication:
>
> Publishing company.
>
> Author's last name, first initial. (Publication date). Article
>
> title. Periodical title, inclusive pages.

Entries illustrating variations on this basic format follow and are numbered to facilitate reference. To compare these entries with those documented in MLA style, refer to the page and item numbers given in brackets.

A Book by One Author

> 1. Boorstin, D. (1992). The creators: A history of the
>
> heroes of the imagination. New York: Random House.
>
> [7,1]

Two or More Books by the Same Author

> 2. Garreau, J. (1981). The nine nations of North America.
>
> Boston: Houghton Mifflin.   [8,3]

3. Garreau, J. (1991). Edge city: Life on the new frontier.

New York: Doubleday.   [8,2]

A Book by More Than One Author

4. Belenky, M. F., Clichy, B. M., Goldberger, N. R., &

Torule, J. M. (1986). Women's ways of knowing: The

development of self, voice, and mind. New York: Basic

Books.   [8,6]

A Book by a Corporate Author

5. Boston Women's Health Book Collective. (1973). Our

bodies, ourselves: A book by and for women. New

York: Simon.   [8,7]

A Work in an Anthology

6. Silko, L. M. (1991). The man to send rain clouds. In W.

Brown and A. Ling (Eds.), Imagining America: Stories

from the promised land. New York: Persea.   [9,13]

A Signed Article from a Daily Newspaper

7. Barringer, F. (1993, March 7). Where many elderly

live, signs of the future. The New York Times, p. 12.

[12,28]

An Article from a Weekly or Biweekly Magazine

8. Trillin, C. (1993, February 15). Culture shopping. The

New Yorker, pp. 48–51.   [13,31]

An Article in a Journal with Continuous Pagination

9. Elbow, P. (1993). Ranking, evaluating, and liking:

Sorting out three forms of judgment. College English,

55, 187–206.   [13,32]

CD-ROM: Printed Source or Printed Analogue

10. West, Cornel. (1987). The dilemma of the black

intellectual. [CD-ROM]. Critical Quarterly, 29, 39–52.

From: SilverPlatter File: MLA International

Bibliography Item: 8800011.   [14,38]

Documenting Sources

The following guidelines and examples emphasize the major differences between the APA and MLA styles of documentation.

1. When you are summarizing or paraphrasing a source and do not mention the author's name in your sentence, place the author's name and date of publication in parentheses. Separate each unit of information with a comma.

Fairy tales help children explore the worlds of

forbidden knowledge (Tuan, 1979).

2. When you are quoting and do not mention the author's name in your sentence, place the author's name, date of publication, and page number(s) in parentheses.

Although fairy tales contain frightening information,

they "thrill rather than terrify a healthy child" (Tuan,

1979, p. 20).

3. When you are quoting and you mention the name of the author in your sentence, place only the publication date and page number(s) in parentheses.

> Tuan (1979) suggests that the effect of fairy tales is muted by "the affectionate environment in which the stories are usually told" (p. 20).

4. If you use more than one source written in the same year by the same author, follow the pattern established in your reference list and include the letter assigned to the source.

> (Turnbull, 1965b)

5. If you cite several sources in one place, list them in alphabetical order by authors' last names and separate them with a semicolon.

> The Mbuti Pygmies, carefree and harmonious, have no concept of evil and thus no real sense of fear (Tuan, 1979; Turnbull, 1965a).

References

Tuan, Y. (1979). Landscapes of fear. New York: Pantheon.

Turnbull, C. M. (1965a). The Mbuti Pygmies of the Congo. In J. L. Gibbs, Jr. (Ed.), Peoples of Africa (pp. 281–317). New York: Holt, Rinehart and Winston.

Turnbull, C. M. (1965b). Wayward servants: The two worlds of the African Pygmies. Garden City, N.Y.: Natural History Press.

Index